THE
*Archive Photographs*
SERIES

# HARLOW

THE
*Archive Photographs*
SERIES

# HARLOW

*Compiled by*
George Taylor

**CHALFORD**

First published 1995
Copyright © George Taylor, 1995

The Chalford Publishing Company
St Mary's Mill, Chalford,
Stroud, Gloucestershire, GL6 8NX

ISBN 0 7524 0330 3

Typesetting and origination by
The Chalford Publishing Company
Printed in Great Britain by
Redwood Books, Trowbridge

# Contents

# Introduction

When I moved to Harlow in 1974 as a place to live on impending retirement a friend from Enfield said "Harlow? That concrete jungle!" That was not unfamiliar as a descriptive term by those living in the leafy suburbs of London. However I soon brought him home and as soon as we entered the Harlow area he was quite surprised by the apparent lack of people living on the access roads let alone any sign of concrete jungle. Being by profession an estate agent he covered his obvious embarrassment by muttering how many nice houses he could build in our green wedges! It was a thought which was not lost on me.

Why did I come to Harlow? Around 70 years ago I spent school holidays with my aunt living in a village close to the original town called Harlow which was the nearest civilised place where I could walk to the market and the shops and see a railway and a river. All this and the rural way of life with water from the pump and oil lamps was of lasting interest to a small boy from East London.

The next step was in 1955 when I joined an evening extension course at Chesthunt on the subject of town planning in which I was especially interested. The course arranged visits to Harlow during the period when the new town was really getting going and I recall a lecture by the General Manager on what it was all about.

Last and not least was the fact that my daughter and her husband plus two small grandchildren were living in Harlow in 1974 and my wife and I had had good opportunity to see the pros and cons of the town.

So early in that year we moved and when I retired from full-time work in June we also attended a short course by Katharine Davidson (the curator of the Harlow Museum) on ancient civilisations (a subject of interest and ignorance to us!), and quickly became members of the Friends of the Museum. Before long, as a member of the committee, I was asked to attend the Town Hall at a meeting of voluntary groups concerned with publicity. I was surprised that no one had mentioned photographs; there was no comment but after the meeting I was given a "To whom it may concern" letter by the Head of Information giving authority for access to Council property to take photographs. This has led to many thousands of photographs for the Harlow Development Corporation and Harlow Council on the continued development and activities of the town. My particular subjects were archaeology and history and all subjects of community life which fitted in well with my membership of the Friends of Harlow Museum.

The Master Plan for the new town was based upon the geographical nature of the land selected within the Stort valley surrounded by relatively higher ground. The area includes five parishes which were rich in history from Pre-Roman to Roman times and from the Middle Ages up to the present day. Thus for any "concrete jungle" fraternity still remaining, the Harlow Council in 1981 published a list of 151 listed buildings in the area. The existence of the Harlow Temple was well known but there were further Roman sites for excavation.

An interesting personal note on the period of early human occupation was when I started digging my garden in 1974 and turned up a flint artefact which was identified as a scraper for cleaning animal skins from about 3000 BC. This gave much encouragement to my gardening! The score up to now is over 70 authenticated scrapers which are beautifully made to do this job and fit all sizes of thumb.

The individual parish boundaries were first based upon each parish having access to the river, the water meadow, and up to the higher ground. The object of the Master Plan was to combine them in to a large new town of 60,000 people. At the same time the rural and historic character was to be safeguarded as much as possible as can be seen by the green wedges and wealth of ancient buildings. The town centre was based upon a new site which had room for expansion and changes have also taken place during more recent years.

For an authoritive and detailed account of the town's developement, the book entitled "Harlow, The Story of a New Town" should be consulted. It was written by Sir Frederick Gibberd and colleagues from the Harlow Development Corporation and covers the period from 1947 to 1980 when the Corporation was dissolved. For the progress of archeological studies publications by Harlow Museum and other authorities are available.

Harlow is one of the satellite towns around London which were planned to provide for the overspill caused by the effects of the 1939-45 War. It was natural when the new houses and factories were set up, the east and north-east London suburbs provided a high proportion of the newcomers. They tended to retain their old loyalties which included their way of speech so we had Hackney and Newham days when retired people could meet old neighbours and civic heads.

Archaeological excavations, the preservation and restoration of listed buildings and the accommodation of all the generations in a new town has provided a wealth of photographic material, a sample of which is presented in this book. My experiences confirmed the saying by local historians that history is being made every day especially if it takes the people and the community into account which this collection has tried to do.

## One
# Before the New Town

High Street, Harlow, looking east *c.* 1900. It looked like this to me in the 1920's although there was more, still mainly horse-drawn, traffic.

Station Road looking north *c.* 1900. In the 1920's I was more interested in the market in Fore Street to the left and on the road to Burnt Mill.

The ford across the Harlow Brook *c.* 1900, on the road from Harlow to Sheering connecting Mulberry Green with Churchgate Street. The low buildings on the left are the Reeves almshouses, founded under the will of Francis Reeve who died in 1639. The large building was known in recent times as Colonel Drake's house. The ford was eliminated in 1904 by a bridge built by Essex County Council.

The workers building a factory in 1880 for the Kirkcaldy Marine Engineering Company on the site of the disused flour mill at Burnt Mill. Part of the original building was incorporated in the Outdoor Pursuits Centre of Harlow.

An unnamed Harlow family *c.* 1900.

Sam Deard's shop in Harlow *c*. 1880 sometimes known as the Bon Marche offering a wide range of goods as seen by the notices on the windows and the tools displayed outside.

This is also the Harlow Brook ford *c.* 1900 but in the opposite direction looking to the west from Sheering to Mulberry Green. The nearest house in the centre became a police station.

Todds Bridge, Great Parndon is typical of the fords which were common in the area before there was enough traffic to justify the expense of building a bridge for more than foot travellers and cyclists. At this point there is now a culvert over which passes heavy traffic along the Third Avenue route.

The Ford, Parndon

The baker is watering his horse at the ford before the climb up to the cottages and school by the church of St Mary of Great Parndon.

I was showing a slide of this Little Parndon Choir of 1910 to a community audience when someone spoke up and said he was one of the small choristers to the left.

This was the next slide showing the first aeroplane seen in Harlow in 1912 piloted by Claud Graham-White and the same informant told us that despite the appearance of a well-to-do local population the locals had been given plenty of time to go home and put on their Sunday best clothes before the picture was taken.

This is the Round House or Crutch House in 1910 where my friend lived. He told me that he became a plasterer earning 1s 3d per hour locally but 3d more if he cycled to Bow in London. The house was demolished when the new town expanded to Latton and Potter Street.

The Clock Tower, Latton St.                    B Pavitt, Potters Street, Harlow

The Clock Tower was preserved when the new town included Latton Street. One of our community friends told me how he had climbed up the Tower to wind up the clock.

The Green Man in Mulberry Green was a popular place for the Essex Hunt to meet as in this scene c. 1920.

The Greyhound, Netteswell *c.* 1910. The shop on the left was a butcher's shop and the site became the premises of the Youth Hostel Association. The pond in the foreground is now the site of the entrance to the car park for visitors to the town park.

This is Elizabeth, my sister, in a rowing boat on the Stort hired at Harlow in 1926. It is typical of the fairly elaborate skiffs designed and probably made at Cambridge.

Before the days of herbicides in 1924 one could pick an assortment of wildflowers on the edges of the cornfields around Harlow. The picture shows me on the right with my school friend Claude Leonard and my sister Florence at a field which was a mile or so from where Harlow Town Station now stands.

This is Elizabeth in 1926 on the bridge over the Stort where the town park now extends.

In 1926 this ford at Great Parndon, known as the 'Parndon Splash', was where Elizabeth photographed Wilfred Hazell. He is smoking a pipe which seemed a necessary prop at that time if you were having your photograph taken informally -or failing a pipe then a cigarette judging by the family albums of the time. Wilfred became my brother-in-law and lived until recently to the age of 94. Elizabeth is now 94.

The Victoria Hall in 1930 upon the occasion of a carnival which seemed popular and well attended.

The Harlow Bowling Club in 1932 displaying the bowls and their funny hats.

Another carnival in the same period displaying some well made up characters as the 'Inkspots' and Charlie Chaplin.

A popular 'dressing-up' for carnivals was girls of all nations or other easily recognised subjects as in this group of competitors in Harlow *c*. 1932.

The Home Guard in Netteswell *c*. 1943.

The final parade of the Home Guard at Mulberry Green in 1945. In another place I was in a similar parade followed by a farewell supper.

*Two*

# The New Town
# Develops

The Minister of Town and Country Planning, Lewis Silkin, announces over the BBC, on 25 March 1947, the order of designation for a planned community of 60,000 people to the west of the village of Harlow.

Mr Frederick Gibberd, appointed as the Master Planner, visits Harlow to meet the local councillors.

# NETTESWELL PARISH COUNCIL.

— A —

# PARISH MEETING

will be held on

## THURSDAY, JULY 17th

At 7.30 p.m.,

In the

## W.I. HALL, NETTESWELL.

## Mr. FREDERICK GIBBERD

will give an explanation of the
Harlow New Town Plan, with Maps on view.

MEMBERS OF THE HARLOW NEW TOWN CORPORATION
will be present.

*The Meeting will be quite informal.*

**Chairman: Mr. E. D. WOODLAND.**

RESIDENTS OF LATTON ARE INVITED.

The Harlow Printing Company Ltd., Harlow.

The notice of the meeting of the Netteswell Parish to which residents of Latton are also invited
to hear Mr Gibberd give an explanation of the Harlow New Town Plan.

A reunion meeting of Sir Frederick Gibberd and Mr Ted Woodland, the speaker and Chairman of the Netteswell Parish in 1947, during the formal opening of the Leah Manning Centre in October 1980. I knew both gentlemen and there was no problem getting an informal photograph.

Sir Frederick had pleasure in opening his extensive gardens on behalf of the United Nations Association which were the occasions for international dancing displays.

An attraction of the Gibberd gardens was this splendid avenue of trees. Sir Frederick was said to be the only Master Planner who actually lived within the designated area of planning.

Dick Relf, the Chief Estates Officer, handed over the first house keys to Mr Satchell on 4 August 1949.

A scene at the Harvey Centre in 1977 as part of the exhibition to celebrate the 40th Anniversary of the designation of the new town of Harlow. Mr and Mrs Satchell, the first tenant residents, are being televised for the occasion.

The Harlow Urban District Council was created in 1955 when the population had reached 24,000 of whom 1 in 5 were under school age. The Council's Coat of Arms was unveiled in the market square by Lord Silkin in 1957 with Councillor Don Anderson, Chairman of Council, presiding.

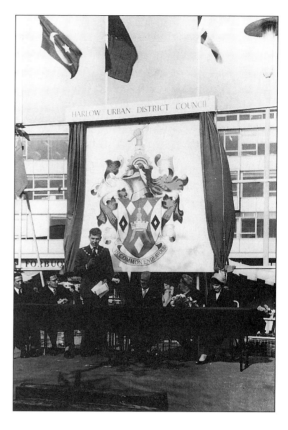

A model was demonstrated of the town centre in the early 1960s. This view was taken from the north to south line of the model.

The visit of the Queen and the Duke of Edinburgh to the High in October 1957.

Part of the crowd welcoming the royal visit.

The Duke of Edinburgh visits Moot House with Sir Richard Costain.

The opening of the Swimming Pool in August 1961. Councillor E W Buckle, Chairman of the Council, Christopher Mayhew MP, in place of Lord Dalton who was unwell, and Councillor Bill Fisher. The fanfare was by State Trumpeters of the Life Guards.

Harold Macmillan Prime Minister visiting Harlow in 1959 with Raymond Thompson, Ben Hyde Harvey, T.H. Joyce and Richard Costain.

Lord Attlee opening the first stage of the building of Harlow Town Hall in 1960.

An early record of the members of the resident Alberni Quartet who were from left to right: Dennis Simons, Gregory Baron, John White, Howard Davis in 1963.

An early Scout Cub group *c.* 1960 off School Lane.

Roller skating was very popular c. 1960 and this group was enjoying its sport in the Moot Hall.

Country dancing in Harlow c. 1955.

The opening by Harlow Development Corporation of Moot Hall as part of the community centre in 1952.

The growth of the new town was based upon the development of local industries but in January 1968 the workers at an engineering plant were faced with losing their jobs because of a take-over bid, despite having received a Queen's Award for the excellence of their work. Hence the protest march of more than 800 led by the local MP, Stan Newens and Chairman of the Council, Jock Arnott.

Hackney Day at the Leah Manning Centre in 1981 showing Alex James, Chairman of Harlow Council with the Mayor of Hackney, Councillor Martin Ottolangui, and Stan Newens MP. On the board are the names of the streets in Hackney where present citizens of Harlow formerly lived. This helped old neighbours to meet again.

Hackney Day - serving out dishes of jellied eels to remind citizens of customs of the old days.

Newham Day with the Chairman of Harlow Council, Laurie Smith, Ron Bill, who organised the special days, and the Mayor of Newham. An exhibition of old photographs of Newham had been assembled. Laurie Smith told me his family forbears had let out their horses on Plaistow marshes in West Ham.

Harlow Day 1982 where those who had lived in the area before the new town could meet old friends. Stan Newens MP, who had continued to live in the Old Harlow part, is describing the history including that of the hand bells on display.

A substantial increase in housing started in 1976 at Katherines against the background of St Mary's church, Great Parndon.

Modern methods of using pre-formed components were put into practice in the Katherines and Sumners areas from 1976.

The blend of the new town housing at Five Acres in 1980 with the green wedges and the old oak tree. Lord Dalton had written "New Towns are one of our greatest social inventions and Harlow has always been one of the outstanding examples as a thriving, happy community with many marks of distinction and originality".

From the same vantage point can be seen the Goldings farm house and buildings dating from the fifteenth Century and modified in the nineteenth Century with the Harlow Town Centre and high-rise flats in the distance.

The new housing at Guilfords, completed in 1977, provides the background to the tree at the entrance to Harlowbury and the wall of Harlowbury Chapel with their twelfth Century associations.

The planning of Harlow included the retention of old trees as much as possible but by 1980, some had outlived their useful lives and were becoming dangerous. This one is being removed in Rectory Lane Great Parndon. Other trees had been attacked by Dutch Elm Disease since 1970 and this had altered the landscape.

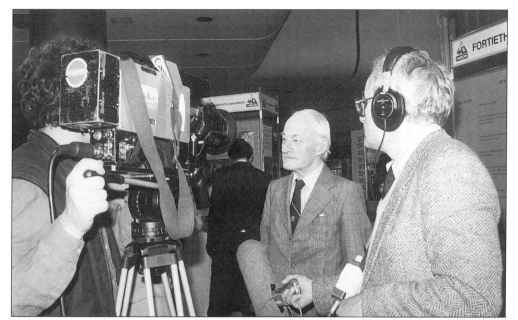

Mr Ben Hyde Harvey, who had made important contributions to the success of Harlow and in recognition of whom the Harvey Centre was named, is being interviewed by Thames TV during his visit to the 40th anniversary exhibition in the Centre in 1987.

The 40th anniversary was marked by many displays and projects by the children including the 'Harlow Story' presentation.

I photographed this gathering at the steps in the Town Hall to celebrate the 40th anniversary. Many of the Councillors were there and the Chairman, Laurie Smith, is on the left with Lady Gibberd. Stan Newens MEP and Dermot Byrne are in the group.

The Chairman of the Council, Councillor Mike Danvers, speaking to the people who had come to see the opening of a recent housing development in the Churchgate Street area of the town in 1987.

Mrs Fitzwilliam performing the opening ceremony in 1987 for the naming of Fitzwilliam Court as a tribute to her family's long interest and contribution to the developments in Churchgate Street.

In another part of the town at the neighbourhood of Staple Tye. The shopping centre seen in May 1977 was to be demolished in the early 1990s and replaced by a new centre entirely at ground floor level. The growth of car ownership was not foreseen in 1947 and this has led to out of town supermarkets in former industrial areas.

Industrial development is still proceeding in 1995 with the erection of tower cranes for the new buildings for an expanding drug company in the Pinnacles industrial area.

*Three*

# Town Centre

The opening of the market in May-June 1956. The inspector was given an office in the caravan with a board outside so that the day of the next market could be chalked. The advertisements are typical of the times.

The market was well developed and busy in 1965 and even the trees had grown.

By 1960 the town had a high proportion of babies and was justifiably called 'Pram Town' as this scene from the Broad Walk shows.

The town had attracted many well known national shops. Prominent was Marks and Spencers which at that time was opposite Woolworths. It is still there in 1995 but the interior scene may be less familiar.

Civic Square on a wet day in 1976 when there was a temporary building opposite occupied by the Co-op.

The same wet day looking south across the water gardens with housing and Passmores School in the distance across a green wedge.

A night shot at the time of the Christmas lights along the Broad Walk looking north in 1979.

A musical group at practice in St Paul's church the new church of the new town. I was told by Canon Knight, the first vicar, that he brought to St Paul's and installed the bells of the war damaged church of the Holy Trinity, Canning Town to signify the association of the East End with Harlow New Town. On a personal note, I was christened at Holy Trinity church in 1913.

A scene of activity by patrons of the Playhouse theatre in 1978.

In August 1978 Roy Hattersley MP, who was Secretary of State for Prices and Consumer Protection, opened the Advice Centre in Harlow with John Moore, Chairman of Council.

The Family Group sculpture by Henry Moore at the spot he chose from several positions he had inspected. Since then because of vandalism and the effects of the weather it has had to be repaired and awaits a new location with more protection. At the time of this photograph in 1979, the extension to the library and the snooker centre was being built.

A different view of the market as it was in 1981.

Also in 1981 and with the temporary covers over the stalls, is the activity at the Broad Walk side of the market.

54

By the next year the permanent covers were in place and the informal and varied attitudes of the stallholders and their customers and those 'just looking around' could be recorded from above.

The Welfare Rights team were celebrating their 10th anniversary in 1985 with Councillor Rene Morris cutting the cake in the Harvey Centre.

The construction of the obelisk in Broad Walk in 1980 as a monument to the Harlow Development Corporation in planning and developing the new town.

The construction of the new buildings which offered new shops and offices at the south end of Broad Walk at a site left vacant is well underway in September 1986.

The Planning Group photographed in 1987 with a panoramic view to the west of the Town Hall.

Chairman of the Council, Laurie Smith and Mrs Smith talking to Ted Witt and John Bowers on the 30th anniversary of the opening of the market in 1956.

It was also an occasion to meet some younger citizens of Harlow.

The Technical College by night in 1976.

A night shot of the town centre looking north in 1976.

The Tesco building under construction in 1981.

The final stages in the construction of the Boots building in 1987.

# *Four*
# Historic Buildings

In June 1976, the walk of the Friends of Harlow Museum was across the site of the deserted medieval village towards the house of Harlowbury with farm buildings on the right and Harlowbury chapel with its roof much in need of repair on the left. The Friends campaigned to put this right as appropriate for a Class 1 listed building dating back to the twelfth Century.

The nineteenth Century brick built cladding of Harlowbury House gave a false impression of the age of the structure but the interest of the new owners Mr and Mrs Toettcher led to the discovery of a far earlier building. This can be seen by the carved crown post and other details being examined by John Collins and Barry Foley of the Friends in 1982.

The main part of the roof space being examined to see the blackened timbers where the smoke got out through a hole in the roof before the days of chimneys.

Adrian Gibson, a member of the research group, with Cecil Hewitt and John McCann describing how the medieval house of Harlowbury had been constructed.

The model on the right is how the original Harlowbury Chapel is believed to have been with the left model representing its conversion and use as a granary possibly from the seventeenth century.

Members of the Harlow Amenity and Conservation Society (HACS) viewing the chapel before restoration in 1982. In the centre is Neils Toettcher the new owner.

At an early stage in the restoration, part of the roof had been removed showing by daylight the elegance of construction and carving of the crown posts.

In 1982 HACS won joint second prize in the Civic Trust 'Pride of Place' competition for the chapel project and an award of £1,000 started off the funding of the restoration of Harlow's most important historic building. For the presentation of the certificate is Miss Knightley daughter of the founder of the competition with Katharine Chant Chairman of HACS and a group of young musicians with early instruments trained and led by Ernie Norris.

Stone masons of the Strachey firm at work in 1983 in restoring the windows at the east end of the chapel which had been blocked when it had been converted to a granary.

A fundraising event at the chapel in 1983.

Another fundraising event with musicians and dancing in the yard between Harlowbury House and farm buildings. Eventually the money was raised to complete the restoration although need still exists for maintenance of the building. During investigation of the floor evidence of an earlier structure was found by earlier post holes shown by carbon dating to be eighth century.

As the new town developed not all the ancient churches were sited in the areas of the new population thus St Andrew's at Netteswell was declared redundant and this is the last service conducted by the Rev Richard Bray looking east on St Andrew's Day on 30 November 1983.

The same scene looking west.

Brasses from the seventeenth Century preserved in St Andrew's. John Bannister was a deacon in the parish of Netteswell.

A new church St Stephen's, was built in Tye Green to replace St Andrew's and this informal record of part of the congregation was made at the request of Rev Bray and a very large print placed in the entrance hall of St Stephen's.

Woodbine Cottages at Linford End with Bessie Wallis at the door. A group of three workers' cottages needing repair and restoration and the new owner of the site had permission to convert them to a single spacious house.

Dismantling and repair in progress by Richard Dorsett in 1981.

Details of the original construction being examined by the new owners Robin and Irma Hall and members of HACS.

At the launch of the new book 'Parndon Recollections' at Harlow Museum on 20 October 1980 with the author Jim Priest on the left with Christopher Taylor (who wrote the foreword), Stan Newens and Lady Gibberd. Jim was born in one of the Woodbine Cottages.

The Great Parndon new bell number two being guided up the church tower of St Mary's by David Aarons in December 1979.

The ancient tithe barn of Netteswellbury in 1989 being refurbished to renew the roof much damaged by a fire. This was part of the extensive development of the whole site including other smaller barns and St Andrew's church which was completed as a visitors and study centre and warden-assisted accommodation.

*Five*

# Community

Archaeological work being undertaken at the Staffords site by voluntary workers in August 1980.

Work on the Harlow Temple site in 1985 examining the soil surface for remains of artefacts hence the heads down posture!

Richard Bartlett of Harlow Museum supervising the Temple site investigations, with the head of Minerva of Roman origin recovered.

Richard in the laboratory of the Museum explaining the process of conservation of artefacts to two young observers.

Harlow Museum Open Day in May 1976 with a jazz band entertaining visitors.

Harlow Town Band at the Open Day in May 1978.

St George's Canzona giving a performance with their Medieval-type instruments at the Museum in 1987.

A hand bells demonstration at the Museum Open Day in 1978.

'Morris Minor' in the display of morris dancing in 1987.

On a previous occasion in better weather in May 1977. The morris dancing is hailed by a caller before a relaxed audience at Harlow Museum.

Entertainments by the Barbershop Quartet consisting of Kevin Corrigan, Bob Mallison, Roger Wardle and David Lavery from left to right, in 1978.

Harlow Museum arranged many children's events with an historical theme giving an opportunity to dress up in the costume appropriate for the time. This is a Tudor Day crowd being treated to a juggling display in 1982.

The old Mark Hall stable block being repaired and rebuilt to the requirements of a modern cycle museum in 1980.

Conversion completed and exhibits displayed in the new gallery in 1982. A Civic Trust Award was granted to the project.

The south side of the new museum topped by the original bell tower which had had to be extensively repaired in 1982.

Robin Bletsoe describing to the Council committee the plans in 1981 for giving a new lease of life to the walled gardens of the Cycle Museum which had previously been productive for the old Mark Hall estate.

Lady Jeger unveiling the sculpture of Leah Manning and shaking hands with the sculptor Christopher Dean in a ceremony for the new Leah Manning Day Centre for retired citizens of Harlow.

Two members of the Old Harlow Glee Club having a quiet cup of tea after giving a performance at the Leah Manning Centre in 1980.

Helping hands for a working session at the Centre in 1980.

The snooker table has always been a popular attraction for the retired men coming to the Centre.

A quiet game of cards at the Aneurin Bevan Centre in Old Harlow in 1983.

A musical interlude at St Michael's Close, a sheltered housing unit at Netteswell.

Harlow Council has always recruited and paid tribute to the work of voluntary wardens and this is voluntary warden Mrs Ball talking to one of the residents whilst on her rounds in Peterswood.

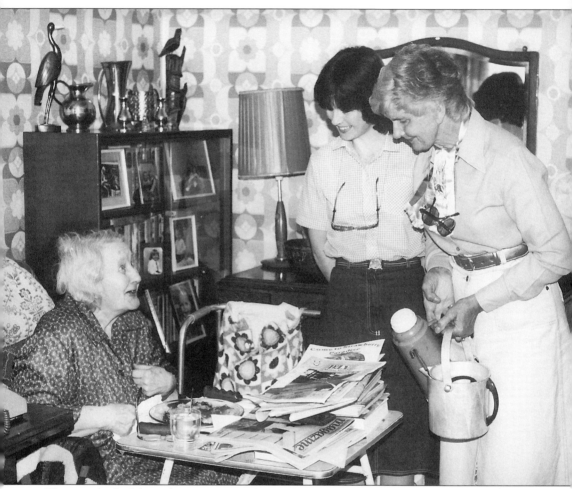

This is typical of the welcome given to the Meals-on-Wheels team of Dolores and Vi visiting a client in 1982 in Jerounds, Great Parndon.

*Six*
# Transport

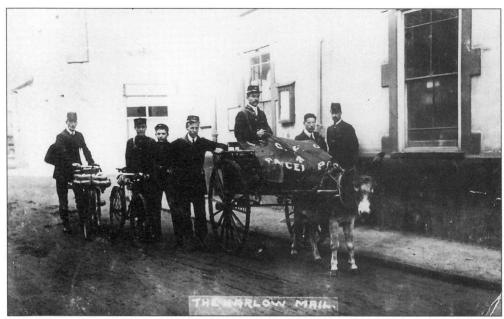

The Harlow Mail in 1909 with a donkey cart supported by a bicycle squad.

Char-a-banc outing from Great Parndon *c.* 1920.

Young horse riders under instruction in the Town Park in 1980.

Mr Green from Holloway who retired at the same time as his horse in 1953 upon the occasion of the last horse-drawn barge journey on the Stort-Lee canal system. He told me that he walked over 30 miles per day and did not wear socks inside his heavy boots.

The last lock at Waltham Abbey showing the magnificent animal bred for use on canal tow paths that is short in height to work low bridges and very powerful in legs and shoulders to pull the heavy barges. Mr Green also told me with pride that his horse had pulled out the newly introduced tractors when they had got stuck.

The narrow boats can still be used on the Stort for pleasure and instructional purposes. This one, the 'Young Tudor Rose', is being used by me for instruction in photography for Harlow Adult Education in 1983.

A genuine example of the English Boneshaker (1869) which preceded the modern bicycle on display in the Mark Hall Cycle Museum Gallery Five. It had a sprung saddle and a brake of sorts and its name can be believed judging by the thin solid tyres. It was propelled by the scooting action of legs and feet on the ground.

The Collins family cycle shop was an institution for many years in Harlow and this is the workshop with Hugh White, the mechanic, in 1971, before the shop was turned into domestic housing as legally required when John retired from keeping the family business.

John Collins displaying his penny-farthing at the Open Day at Harlow Museum in 1979.

Veteran Cycle Club members approaching the Cycle Museum in an event held in 1984.

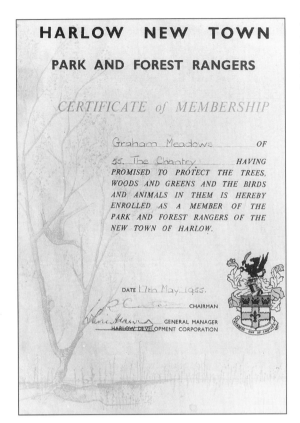

The certificate of membership of the Harlow New Town Park and Forest Rangers issued to Graham Meadows in May 1955 and signed by Richard Costain and Ben Hyde Harvey.

The Park and Forest Rangers on parade with their motorcycles at the Stow in 1955.

Nurse Lee, the district nurse from Hunsdon. I knew Nurse Lee who was a much appreciated member of her profession. I think this Douglas motorcycle was owned by the local vicar and Nurse Lee did her rounds on a bicycle. The original print was from Mrs Jordan and the Hunsdon Local History Society.

At the Harlow Museum Open Day in 1979 a number of motorcycles were exhibited including my L E Velocette. This water-cooled shaft drive machine was once widely used by rural police, its almost noiseless approach helping to catch poachers. I owned five over the years.

Burnt Mill Station before its site was taken and used by the Harlow Development Corporation in 1960 for the new Harlow Town station.

When Harlow New Town was planned it was hoped that most of the residents would live and work in the town probably cycling to and from work on the cycle ways. Nevertheless Harlow Town station continued to be and still is the main connection for commuters to London. This is the first passenger off a commuting train from London in 1978.

A line of commuters checking their coinage for the exact fare on the bus in 1978. The background has changed with office blocks there now.

For workers in Harlow factories the bus was an alternative to cycling or later to using a car. This is a 5pm scene in January 1977 at the Pinnacles with a bus going to Harlow Mill station which used to be called Harlow station before the new town came.

A Ford veteran car on display at Harlow Museum Open Day in 1976. This print was exhibited with the title 'Wheels' -how many can you see? I had a picnic trip in a Model T Ford newly acquired by my uncle Tom Brown of Deptford c. 1919. I was looked after by my mother and remember that she was asked to look out the back for blue smoke to check that the oil was getting through.

The taxi rank at the bus station terminus in 1977 before the area was replanned and alterations started. This was called 'Rank Outsider' not from the mini in the foreground but from the white taxi inching its way on to the rank.

*Seven*

# The Young

Great Parndon school photograph of 1910 with two daughters of the Chalk family, the taller one in the middle of the back row and her younger sister second from the left in the middle row. In recent years they occupied adjacent old peoples' bungalow in Jerounds and with the help of the voluntary warden they were kind enough to give an account of their earlier lives which I recorded on tape for Harlow Museum.

This photograph, together with the two following, shows pupils of Fawbert and Barnard School in the early 1930s. We have key plans with names. They are examples of archive records which have been of sustained interest to the 'Memories Group' set up by Evelyn Salisbury, manager of the Neighbourhood Office of Old Harlow.

There are relatives of the families still living in Harlow. Interesting developments have visits by 'Memories Group' members to the school, which is still running under its original name, and return visits of present day pupils to the Group at the Aneurin Bevan Centre.

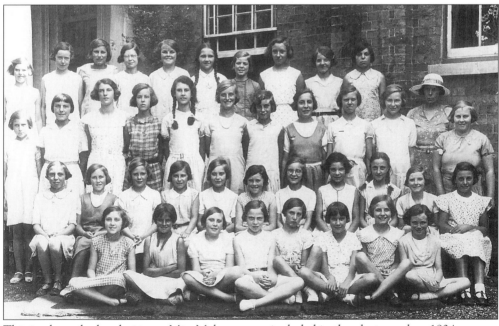

This is where the headmistress, Miss Maloney, was included in the photograph *c.* 1934.

Harlow Council's pre-school group in Kingsmoor House, 1984.

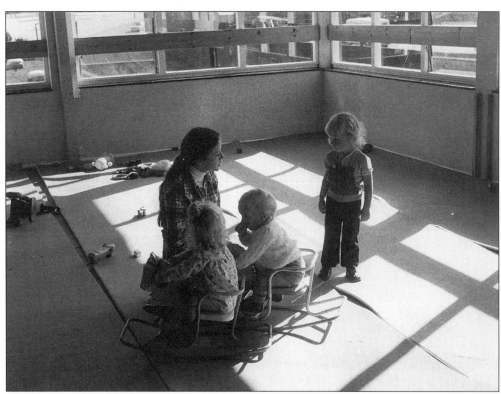

Taking care of young children in the Sportscentre in 1979 when their mothers were enjoying the facilities offered for sports and training.

In March 1978, when the new school at Katherines was operational, the Harlow Development Corporation, through its Social Development Officer, asked me to provide examples of the Open Plan in operation. This is where early arithmetic was being taught by the help of the dice although one parent on seeing this print said "I send my child to school to learn and not to play!" but this remark may not have been meant seriously.

Part of the same exercise in Open Plan, this is a modelling class at work. It will be appreciated that for this type of record the photographer must be ignored by the children.

Active play at 'the shop' in the temporary building set up in Katherines in 1983.

The 3K's Club, as they called themselves, in August 1983.

The shop from the customers' side.

A play group being provided at Rivermill during the school holidays, August 1979. It is hoped that they were able to help their mothers make the pastry after this.

The Toddlers Race by St Nicholas' School near Churchgate Street. Encouragement experienced and enjoyed by the parents in 1977.

St Nicholas' School pupils on the ski slope at Harlow in 1977. Their tracks can be seen in the frost.

The immediate post-war period being enacted at the Visitors and Study Centre by dressing up and enjoying the rock and roll session.

At the re-enactment, sweets of the time being weighed out by Sandra against coupons from ration books in a suitable weighing machine and weights.

The Netteswell Youth Band at full blast at a display in the town park on Senior Citizens Day July 1982.

A pupil rushes from Abbotsweld School in July 1977.

# Eight

# Sport, Leisure and Impressions

This was probably the first bowling facility offered by the new town *c*. 1958.

A more recent sport of skateboarding taking off near the town centre in 1979.

The provision for all kinds of indoor sports at the Sportcentre with galleries for spectators in 1979.

Marathon runners approaching the finish along Fifth Avenue in 1974.

Football was probably the most popular team game and pitches and changing rooms were provided in many parts of the new town. This is at Rectory Field in 1975 and my notes refer to Takely FC as the visitors.

At the Harlow Rugby Club near Little Parndon church off Elizabeth Way. The match was the occasion when a Czech team was part of a town twinning exchange group visiting Harlow. The visitors are in the striped jerseys. Earlier that day I photographed a joint ceremony of the planting of a peace tree in the Town Park.

A Chinese dragon dance being given by students of Harlow College in 1987.

Being a tutor in photography, I was asked by the Adult Education Officer in Harlow to photograph other Adult Education subjects for the record and reports. This is from an

instruction in karate held in Burnt Mill School in 1987 with the title 'On Guard'.

The extension of theatre facilities at Harlow College East Site in 1986 was marked by invitations to celebrities of interest to students. Here are Billy Bragg and Attila the Stockbroker performing during their visit to the College.

Senior Citizens' Day in the Town Park in July 1982.

In pursuit of Adult Education classes being recorded to show students profiting by language instruction, this is Pam Houghton, a teacher of French with students in May 1978.

Interest in the cattle and horses competitors in the Harlow Town Show in August 1976.

On the cycle track and footpath to Staple Tye on a bright morning after snowfall in December 1981.

Some quiet fishing in the Stort near Harlow Mill.

A conservation group of volunteers assisting in the coppicing programme at the Harlow Nature Reserve in 1984.

This bee orchid was photographed on the fringe of an industrial estate in Harlow in 1983. Nature has provided this plant with not only the appearance of the bee but also the scent to attact live bees to settle on the flowers to assist pollination of the species.

A pleasure boat being guided through a lock in Harlow.

Photographers at work on the small creatures including rare newts arranged by the warden Vyvyan Veal in the laboratory/library of the Harlow Nature Reserve in 1986.

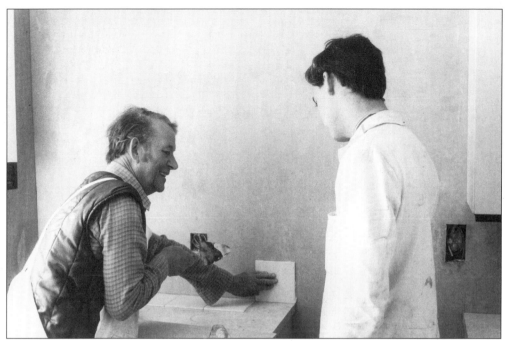

Harlow Council has organised training courses for apprentices in various useful trades which I was asked to record. This is the art of tiling being demonstrated in 1986.

An apprentice plasterer enjoying his work in 1986.

Enjoying a swing in the surroundings of Rectory Field Great Parndon in 1978.

In the new town an industrial estate has extended to the boundary of an ancient monument. This is a modern factory for IDV (Gilbeys) adjacent to the Harlow Temple site. From this angle the sign does not seem to fit.

The cycle and pedestrian way is part of the cycle and footway network underneath Abercrombie Way near Harlow Museum.

Rose Little in her old-fashioned general shop which she has maintained for many years with the help of her daughter just beyond the western border of Harlow. She was awarded the BEM for dealing effectively with a young intruder. She came originally from West Ham and we both went to the same school.

A view of Harlow on a frosty morning in December 1975.

The underpass leading to the market and the town centre and, more recently, to and from Sainsbury's new supermarket on the former Gilbey's site.

The way to Staple Tye shopping precinct on a misty morning with the sun just breaking through in December 1976. All this has now disappeared with the new shops on ground level.

At the Town Show in August 1977. I was asked by the Information Officer of Harlow Council to take pictures of visitors enjoying themselves. Unfortunately as the day dawned it was pouring with rain and so it continued. I reckoned that it was only at the beer tent would I find anyone

looking happy and this was as near to my objective that I could get although some wet children trying to get under the cover set off my happy visitor.

Spin-off from the roundabout feature of the play area in 1978.

# Acknowledgements

Permission is gratefully acknowledged to Harlow Council to use archive material. It has been a pleasure to work with members of Council staff to conserve originals, and to produce new photographs for reports, lectures and exhibitions.

The original print of Nurse Lee was kindly loaned from Mrs Jordan and the Hunsdon Local History Society.

I have made all the prints from my own negatives available for future archive use.

I acknowledge the kind help given to verify the information on the titles by Joyce Jones and Ron Bill each with long and enthusiastic knowledge of the development of Harlow and its community life.

Finally, thanks to may granddaughter, Jo for typing the text.

# Stock List

(Titles are listed according to the pre-1974 county boundaries)

## BERKSHIRE

**Wantage**
*Irene Hancock*
ISBN 0-7524-0146 7

## CARDIGANSHIRE

**Aberaeron and Mid Ceredigion**
*William Howells*
ISBN 0-7524-0106-8

## CHESHIRE

**Ashton-under-Lyne and Mossley**
*Alice Lock*
ISBN 0-7524-0164-5

**Around Bebington**
*Pat O'Brien*
ISBN 0-7524-0121-1

**Crewe**
*Brian Edge*
ISBN 0-7524-0052-5

**Frodsham and Helsby**
*Frodsham and District Local History Group*
ISBN 0-7524-0161-0

**Macclesfield Silk**
*Moira Stevenson and Louanne Collins*
ISBN 0-7524-0315 X

**Marple**
*Steve Cliffe*
ISBN 0-7524-0316-8

**Runcorn**
*Bert Starkey*
ISBN 0-7524-0025-8

**Warrington**
*Janice Hayes*
ISBN 0-7524-0040-1

**West Kirby to Hoylake**
*Jim O'Neil*
ISBN 0-7524-0024-X

**Widnes**
*Anne Hall and the Widnes Historical Society*
ISBN 0-7524-0117-3

## CORNWALL

**Padstow**
*Malcolm McCarthy*
ISBN 0-7524-0033-9

**St Ives Bay**
*Jonathan Holmes*
ISBN 0-7524-0186-6

## COUNTY DURHAM

**Bishop Auckland**
*John Land*
ISBN 0-7524-0312-5

**Around Shildon**
*Vera Chapman*
ISBN 0-7524-0115-7

## CUMBERLAND

**Carlisle**
*Dennis Perriam*
ISBN 0-7524-0166-1

## DERBYSHIRE

**Around Alfreton**
*Alfreton and District Heritage Trust*
ISBN 0-7524-0041-X

**Barlborough, Clowne, Creswell and Whitwell**
*Les Yaw*
ISBN 0-7524-0031-2

**Around Bolsover**
*Bernard Haigh*
ISBN 0-7524-0021-5

**Around Derby**
*Alan Champion and Mark Edworthy*
ISBN 0-7524-0020-7

**Long Eaton**
*John Barker*
ISBN 0-7524-0110-6

**Ripley and Codnor**
*David Buxton*
ISBN 0-7524-0042-8

**Shirebrook**
*Geoff Sadler*
ISBN 0-7524-0028-2

**Shirebrook: A Second Selection**
*Geoff Sadler*
ISBN 0-7524-0317-6

## DEVON

**Brixham**
Ted Gosling and Lyn Marshall
ISBN 0-7524-0037-1

**Around Honiton**
Les Berry and Gerald Gosling
ISBN 0-7524-0175-0

**Around Newton Abbot**
Les Berry and Gerald Gosling
ISBN 0-7524-0027-4

**Around Ottery St Mary**
Gerald Gosling and Peter Harris
ISBN 0-7524-0030-4

**Around Sidmouth**
Les Berry and Gerald Gosling
ISBN 0-7524-0137-8

## DORSET

**Around Uplyme and Lyme Regis**
Les Berry and Gerald Gosling
ISBN 0-7524-0044-4

## ESSEX

**Braintree and Bocking**
John and Sandra Adlam and Mark Charlton
ISBN 0-7524-0129-7

**Ilford**
Ian Dowling and Nick Harris
ISBN 0-7524-0050-9

**Ilford: A Second Selection**
Ian Dowling and Nick Harris
ISBN 0-7524-0320-6

**Saffron Walden**
Jean Gumbrell
ISBN 0-7524-0176-9

## GLAMORGAN

**Around Bridgend**
Simon Eckley
ISBN 0-7524-0189-0

**Caerphilly**
Simon Eckley
ISBN 0-7524-0194-7

**Around Kenfig Hill and Pyle**
Keith Morgan
ISBN 0-7524-0314-1

**The County Borough of Merthyr Tydfil**
Carolyn Jacob, Stephen Done and Simon Eckley
ISBN 0-7524-0012-6

**Mountain Ash, Penrhiwceiber and Abercynon**
Bernard Baldwin and Harry Rogers
ISBN 0-7524-0114-9

**Pontypridd**
Simon Eckley
ISBN 0-7524-0017-7

**Rhondda**
Simon Eckley and Emrys Jenkins
ISBN 0-7524-0028-2

**Rhondda: A Second Selection**
Simon Eckley and Emrys Jenkins
ISBN 0-7524-0308-7

**Roath, Splott, and Adamsdown**
Roath Local History Society
ISBN 0-7524-0199-8

## GLOUCESTERSHIRE

**Barnwood, Hucclecote and Brockworth**
Alan Sutton
ISBN 0-7524-0000-2

**Forest to Severn**
Humphrey Phelps
ISBN 0-7524-0008-8

**Filton and the Flying Machine**
Malcolm Hall
ISBN 0-7524-0171-8

**Gloster Aircraft Company**
Derek James
ISBN 0-7524-0038-X

**The City of Gloucester**
Jill Voyce
ISBN 0-7524-0306-0

**Around Nailsworth and Minchinhampton from the Conway Collection**
Howard Beard
ISBN 0-7524-0048-7

**Around Newent**
Tim Ward
ISBN 0-7524-0003-7

**Stroud: Five Stroud Photographers**
Howard Beard, Peter Harris and Wilf Merrett
ISBN 0-7524-0305-2

## HAMPSHIRE

**Gosport**
Ian Edelman
ISBN 0-7524-0300-1

**Winchester from the Sollars Collection**
*John Brimfield*
ISBN 0-7524-0173-4

## HEREFORDSHIRE
**Ross-on-Wye**
*Tom Rigby and Alan Sutton*
ISBN 0-7524-0002-9

## HERTFORDSHIRE
**Buntingford**
*Philip Plumb*
ISBN 0-7524-0170-X

**Hampstead Garden Suburb**
*Mervyn Miller*
ISBN 0-7524-0319-2

**Hemel Hempstead**
*Eve Davis*
ISBN 0-7524-0167-X

**Letchworth**
*Mervyn Miller*
ISBN 0-7524-0318-4

**Welwyn Garden City**
*Angela Eserin*
ISBN 0-7524-0133-5

## KENT
**Hythe**
*Joy Melville and Angela Lewis-Johnson*
ISBN 0-7524-0169-6

**North Thanet Coast**
*Alan Kay*
ISBN 0-7524-0112-2

**Shorts Aircraft**
*Mike Hooks*
ISBN 0-7524-0193-9

## LANCASHIRE
**Lancaster and the Lune Valley**
*Robert Alston*
ISBN 0-7524-0015-0

**Morecambe Bay**
*Robert Alston*
ISBN 0-7524-0163-7

**Manchester**
*Peter Stewart*
ISBN 0-7524-0103-3

## LINCOLNSHIRE
**Louth**
*David Cuppleditch*
ISBN 0-7524-0172-6

**Stamford**
*David Gerard*
ISBN 0-7524-0309-5

## LONDON
(Greater London and Middlesex)
**Battersea and Clapham**
*Patrick Loobey*
ISBN 0-7524-0010-X

**Canning Town**
*Howard Bloch and Nick Harris*
ISBN 0-7524-0057-6

**Chiswick**
*Carolyn and Peter Hammond*
ISBN 0-7524-0001-0

**Forest Gate**
*Nick Harris and Dorcas Sanders*
ISBN 0-7524-0049-5

**Greenwich**
*Barbara Ludlow*
ISBN 0-7524-0045-2

**Highgate and Muswell Hill**
*Joan Schwitzer and Ken Gay*
ISBN 0-7524-0119-X

**Islington**
*Gavin Smith*
ISBN 0-7524-0140-8

**Lewisham**
*John Coulter and Barry Olley*
ISBN 0-7524-0059-2

**Leyton and Leytonstone**
*Keith Romig and Peter Lawrence*
ISBN 0-7524-0158-0

**Newham Dockland**
*Howard Bloch*
ISBN 0-7524-0107-6

**Norwood**
*Nicholas Reed*
ISBN 0-7524-0147-5

**Peckham and Nunhead**
*John D. Beasley*
ISBN 0-7524-0122-X

**Piccadilly Circus**
*David Oxford*
ISBN 0-7524-0196-3

## SURREY

**Around Camberley**
*Ken Clarke*
ISBN 0-7524-0148-3

**Around Cranleigh**
*Michael Miller*
ISBN 0-7524-0143-2

**Epsom and Ewell**
*Richard Essen*
ISBN 0-7524-0111-4

**Farnham by the Wey**
*Jean Parratt*
ISBN 0-7524-0185-8

**Industrious Surrey: Historic Images of the County at Work**
*Chris Shepheard*
ISBN 0-7524-0009-6

**Reigate and Redhill**
*Mary G. Goss*
ISBN 0-7524-0179-3

**Richmond and Kew**
*Richard Essen*
ISBN 0-7524-0145-9

## SUSSEX

**Billingshurst**
*Wendy Lines*
ISBN 0-7524-0301-X

## WARWICKSHIRE

**Central Birmingham 1870–1920**
*Keith Turner*
ISBN 0-7524-0053-3

**Old Harborne**
*Roy Clarke*
ISBN 0-7524-0054-1

## WILTSHIRE

**Malmesbury**
*Dorothy Barnes*
ISBN 0-7524-0177-7

**Great Western Swindon**
*Tim Bryan*
ISBN 0-7524-0153-X

**Midland and South Western Junction Railway**
*Mike Barnsley and Brian Bridgeman*
ISBN 0-7524-0016-9

## WORCESTERSHIRE

**Around Malvern**
*Keith Smith*
ISBN 0-7524-0029-0

## YORKSHIRE
(EAST RIDING)

**Hornsea**
*G.L. Southwell*
ISBN 0-7524-0120-3

## YORKSHIRE
(NORTH RIDING)

**Northallerton**
*Vera Chapman*
ISBN 0-7524-055-X

**Scarborough in the 1970s and 1980s**
*Richard Percy*
ISBN 0-7524-0325-7

## YORKSHIRE
(WEST RIDING)

**Barnsley**
*Barnsley Archive Service*
ISBN 0-7524-0188-2

**Bingley**
*Bingley and District Local History Society*
ISBN 0-7524-0311-7

**Bradford**
*Gary Firth*
ISBN 0-7524-0313-3

**Castleford**
*Wakefield Metropolitan District Council*
ISBN 0-7524-0047-9

**Doncaster**
*Peter Tuffrey*
ISBN 0-7524-0162-9

**Harrogate**
*Malcolm Neesam*
ISBN 0-7524-0154-8

**Holme Valley**
*Peter and Iris Bullock*
ISBN 0-7524-0139-4

**Horsforth**
*Alan Cockroft and Matthew Young*
ISBN 0-7524-0130-0

**Knaresborough**
*Arnold Kellett*
ISBN 0-7524-0131-9

**Around Leeds**
*Matthew Young and Dorothy Payne*
ISBN 0-7524-0168-8

**Penistone**
*Matthew Young and David Hambleton*
ISBN 0-7524-0138-6

**Selby from the William Rawling
Collection**
*Matthew Young*
ISBN 0-7524-0198-X

**Central Sheffield**
*Martin Olive*
ISBN 0-7524-0011-8

**Around Stocksbridge**
*Stocksbridge and District History Society*
ISBN 0-7524-0165-3

TRANSPORT

**Filton and the Flying Machine**
*Malcolm Hall*
ISBN 0-7524-0171-8

**Gloster Aircraft Company**
*Derek James*
ISBN 0-7524-0038-X

**Great Western Swindon**
*Tim Bryan*
ISBN 0-7524-0153-X

**Midland and South Western Junction Railway**
*Mike Barnsley and Brian Bridgeman*
ISBN 0-7524-0016-9

**Shorts Aircraft**
*Mike Hooks*
ISBN 0-7524-0193-9

This stock list shows all titles available in the United Kingdom as at 30 September 1995.

# ORDER FORM

The books in this stock list are available from your local bookshop. Alternatively they are available by mail order at a totally inclusive price of £10.00 per copy.

For overseas orders please add the following postage supplement for each copy ordered:

European Union £0.36 (this includes the Republic of Ireland)
Royal Mail Zone 1 (for example, U.S.A. and Canada) £1.96
Royal Mail Zone 2 (for example, Australia and New Zealand) £2.47

Please note that all of these supplements are actual Royal Mail charges with no profit element to the Chalford Publishing Company. Furthermore, as the Air Mail Printed Papers rate applies, we are restricted from enclosing any personal correspondence other than to indicate the senders name.

Payment can be made by cheque, Visa or Mastercard. Please indicate your method of payment on this order form.

If you are not entirely happy with your purchase you may return it within 30 days of receipt for a full refund.

Please send your order to:

The Chalford Publishing Company,
St Mary's Mill,
Chalford,
Stroud,
Gloucestershire
GL6 8NX

This order form should perforate away from the book. However, if you are reluctant to damage the book in any way we are quite happy to accept a photocopy order form or a letter containing the necessary information.

## PLEASE WRITE CLEARLY USING BLOCK CAPITALS

Name and address of the person ordering the books listed below:

_____

_____

_____  Post code _____

Please also supply your telephone number in case we have difficulty fully understanding your requirements.　　　Tel.: _____ - _____

Name and address of where the books are to be despatched to (if different from above):

_____

_____

_____  Post code _____

Please indicate here if you would like to receive future information on books published by the Chalford Publishing Company.

____ Yes, please put me on your mailing list 　 ____ No, please just send the books ordered below

| Title | ISBN | Quantity |
|---|---|---|
| ........................................................ | 0-7524-_____-___ | _____ |
| ........................................................ | 0-7524-_____-___ | _____ |
| ........................................................ | 0-7524-_____-___ | _____ |
| ........................................................ | 0-7524-_____-___ | _____ |
| ........................................................ | 0-7524-_____-___ | _____ |
| | Total number of books | _____ |

**Cost of books delivered in UK** = Number of books ordered @ £10 each =£ _____

**Overseas postage supplement** (if relevant) 　　　　　　　　 =£ _____

**TOTAL PAYMENT** 　　　　　　　　　　　　　　　　　　 =£ _____

Method of Payment 　　　 ❑ Cheque 　 ❑ Visa 　 ❑ Mastercard 　　 **VISA**

Please make cheques payable to *The Chalford Publishing Company* 　　 MasterCard

Name of Card Holder 　 _____

Card Number ❑❑❑❑❑❑❑❑❑❑❑❑❑❑❑❑❑❑❑

Expiry date 　❑❑ / ❑❑

I authorise payment of £_____ from the above card

Signed _____